the sushi cookbook

the sushi cookbook

a step-by-step guide to this popular Japanese food

katsuji yamamoto
& roger hicks

Kodansha International
New York • Tokyo • London

A QUINTET BOOK

Published in 1999 by Kodansha America, Inc

06 07 08 09 8 7 6 5

Kodansha America, Inc.
575 Lexington Avenue, New York, New York, 10022, USA.

Kodansha International Ltd.
17–14 Otowa 1-chome, Bunkyo-ku, Tokyo 112-8652, Japan

Library of Congress Cataloging-in-Publication Data
Hicks, Roger
The sushi cookbook : a step-by-step guide to this popular
Japanese food/by Roger Hicks and Katsuji Yamamoto.
p. cm.
Includes index.
ISBN-10: 1-56836-300-1 (hc)
ISBN-13: 978-1-56836-300-4 (hc)
1. Cookery (Fish) 2. Sushi I Yamamoto, Katsuji. II. Title.
TX747.H524 1999
641.6'92—dc21 99-30255

This book was designed and produced by
Quintet Publishing Limited
6 Blundell Street
London N7 9BH

Creative Director: **Richard Dewing**
Art Director: **Paula Marchant**
Designers: **Simon Balley and Joanna Hill**
Project Editor: **Amanda Dixon**
Editor: **Lyn Coutts**
Photographers: **Tim Ferguson-Hill, Howard Shooter, and Steve Alley**

Picture Credits
Life File: pages 6(l), 7(b), 8(l), 9(b)
Axiom Photographic Agency: 6(r), 7(t), 16

Thanks to Hana Japanese Restaurant of London for providing the sushi featured on the jacket.

Special thanks to **Kurumi Hayter** for her expertise in all things Japanese.

Material in this book has previously appeared in *Japanese Cooking for Two* by Kurumi Hayter, and *Step-By-Step Sushi* by Katsuji Yamamoto and Roger Hicks.
Typeset in Great Britain by Central Southern Typesetters, Eastbourne
Manufactured in Hong Kong by Regent Publishing Services Ltd.
Printed in Singapore by Star Standard Industries Pte Ltd.

contents

introduction 6

store cupboard staples 10

buying and preparing fish 16

decorative garnishes 23

sushi rice 25
sushi-meshi

chapter 1 soups and stocks 27

chapter 2 finger sushi 31
nigiri-zushi

chapter 3 rolled sushi 51
maki-zushi

chapter 4 fancy sushi 67

glossary 78

index 80

introduction

The cuisine of Japan has enjoyed an unprecedented boom in popularity. In cities around the world, you find not only Japanese restaurants, but also stores where Japanese produce, ingredients, and cooking equipment can be bought, and stores—even supermarkets—that stock ready-prepared Japanese dishes. And most popular of all has been sushi—gorgeously presented, flavorsome nibbly-things that do you, your health, and your palate a power of good.

Sushi bars are popping up everywhere, and sushi is appearing on the menus of non-Japanese restaurants. But despite our familiarity with things sushi, few of us know very much about it. We cannot tell a *maki* from a *temaki*, a *nori* from an *inari*. Well, that is about to change, because this book is the show-and-tell of sushi. Everything you need to know about ingredients, types of sushi, and how to make and present them is here. There is a wide selection of delicious recipes that require no special skills—beyond a little patience—to prepare. Even if this book never makes it to the kitchen, never go to a sushi bar without it!

humble beginnings

It is said, though certainly not confirmed, that sushi was a culinary accident. The pillow of sushi rice was intended only as a way of preserving the pieces of fish laid across it. The rice was discarded before the fish was eaten. But, over time, people acquired a taste for the combination of vinegared rice and fish, and sushi was invented.

Another story—first recorded some 1,200 years ago—has it that the Japanese Emperor was so impressed by a dish of clams served with rice and vinegar, its creator was ordered to produce it regularly. The refined version of this dish was sushi.

Rice paddies overlooked by a traditional Japanese house

Landing salmon from a small fishing boat, Hokkaido

Mount Fuji

Heian-Jingu shrine, Kyoto

sushi at home

To serve sushi at home, copy the etiquette of sushi bars. On your arrival at a sushi bar, you should automatically be given bowls of Japanese horseradish (*wasabi*) and pickled ginger (*gari*), soy sauce, and green tea (*ocha*). In a traditional sushi bar, you would order just a few pieces, then a few more which the sushi chef (*itamae*) would freshly prepare. In ultra-modern sushi bars, the sushi chef prepares dishes and places them on a conveyor belt that runs around the bar. You choose your sushi off the conveyor belt. The best and easiest way to serve at home is to prepare a selection of sushi, arrange it on plates on the table, and then allow your guests to make their own selection. A good meal for one is two pieces of six different types of sushi.

healthy and light

In a nutshell, sushi is a wonderfully healthy food. If you opt to eat fish raw, you will gain the benefits of many trace minerals and vitamins. All sushi, with the exception of egg pancake (*tamago*), is low in cholesterol, and if you are calorie-counting, the average rolled sushi has less than 100 calories.

On the negative side, there are two things to consider: salt and food poisoning. Soy sauce is salty. Though the sodium levels in a modest sushi meal are nothing alarming, you may prefer to lower quantities of soy sauce or use a sodium-reduced soy sauce and salt substitute. Raw fish for sushi and *sashimi* must be absolutely fresh, not only for the

Koi carp kites, Kochi Prefecture

Beautifully presented sushi and *sashimi*

best results, but to prevent a gastronomic event becoming a gastronomic illness. Sushi made with raw salmon is not common in Japan as traditionally salmon is salted and salted salmon is not suitable for sushi. However, parasites are also found in many types of fish, especially salmon. Although freezing is said to kill the parasites and their eggs, buy only the freshest produce from the best purveyors, store it correctly, and be fastidious about hygiene.

types of sushi

Finger sushi (*nigiri-zushi*)—the best-known and simplest form of sushi which became popular as a "fast food" in Japan about 200 years ago. It consists of a topping, smeared with Japanese horseradish, resting on a pillow of rice. Sometimes finger sushi are finished with a strap of seaweed paper. If done correctly, the sushi will stay together when picked up with the fingers or chopsticks.

Box sushi (*hako-zushi*)—preparation requires a pressing box (a shallow, rectangular wooden box with a removable lid and base). The rice is spread to cover the base of the box, smeared with Japanese horseradish, and the topping laid over the rice. The lid is positioned and pressed down to form one large block of "sushi," which is sliced into pieces. Box sushi have most in common with finger sushi.

Rolled sushi (*maki-zushi*)—there are countless varieties of rolled sushi, and each sushi chef creates their own specialties. At its simplest, rolled sushi consists of seaweed paper spread with rice and topped with one

Traditional paper lanterns

or more fillings. It is then rolled tightly using a bamboo rolling mat (*makisu*), and sliced into individual rounds. Small sushi rolls are called *hoso-maki;* large ones with many fillings are *futo-maki.* A rolled sushi where rice forms the outer layer are referred to as inside-out *maki.*

"Battleship" sushi (*gunkan-maki*)—hand-formed sushi that has a wall of seaweed paper surrounding a pillow of rice. The wall contains a topping of soft ingredients like fish roe.

Hand-rolled sushi (*temaki*)—sushi that looks like an old-fashioned ice cream cone or cornet. The seaweed paper is topped with rice and fillings, then rolled by hand into a cornet. Strictly, any sushi that is not pressed with a bamboo mat and is rolled by hand is *temaki.*

Scattered sushi (*chirashi-zushi*)—consists of fish, meat, egg pancake, and vegetables artfully arranged over a bed of sushi rice. Scattered sushi can either be served in individual bowls or in one large bowl for a group to share.

Sashimi—not strictly sushi, but thin slices of raw fish, normally served with a side bowl of rice and accompanied by a bowl of *miso* soup.

Sake barrels

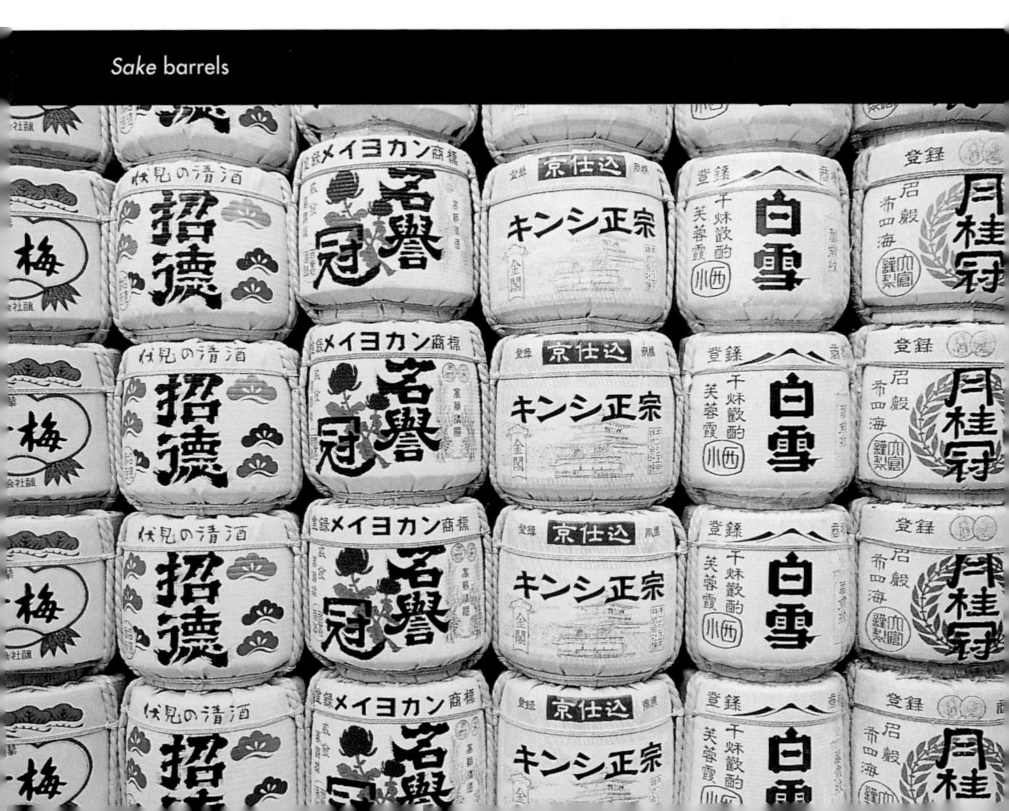

store cupboard staples

Many of the ingredients listed here are now widely available in the West, and can be bought from your local supermarket or grocery store. The rest can be found in Japanese stores and specialty food stores.

Deep-fried bean curd (*abura-age*)

Dried bonito flakes (*katsuo-bushi*)

Fish cake (*kamaboko*)

Fish paste (*oboro*)

Bamboo shoots (*takenoko*)—sold in cans or packaged fresh, bamboo shoots should be eaten as soon as possible after opening. Canned shoots will, however, last for a couple of days in a refrigerator if the water in which they are stored is changed daily.
Bean curd or tofu (*tofu*)—made from soy beans it is creamy-white in color, and its taste is best described as bland. See also Deep-fried bean curd.
Chinese hot pepper paste—made from chiles, fermented soy beans, salt, and sugar, this is one of the most commonly-used sauces in Chinese cuisine and the Chinese name for it is *toban djan*.
Citrus vinegar dressing (*ponzu*)—made from freshly squeezed lemon, lime, or orange juice mixed with soy sauce, vinegar, and a little sugar. It can be bought or made at home by mixing 1/2 cup of orange juice, the juice of 1/2 a lemon, 1/2 cup of soy sauce, and 1/2 cup of Premier Stock (*Dashi*) (see page 28).
Deep-fried bean curd (*abura-age*)—thin, deep-fried pouches of bean curd that are light brown in color with a rough sponge-like texture. It should be frozen or used within a few days of purchase.
Dried bonito flakes (*katsuo-bushi*)—used in making stock, dried bonito fish is traditionally sold in a solid block, which is shaved for use. It can also be bought ready-shaved.
Dried gourd (*kampyō*)—the skin of a Japanese gourd, it is sold in long, dried strips that are reconstituted before use (see page 15). It is used in some kinds of rolled sushi and in scattered sushi.
Dried *shiitake* mushrooms—the most common and flavorful mushroom used in Japanese and Chinese cooking. Dried and fresh *shiitake* mushrooms are widely available, although it is the reconstituted dried form that is often used in sushi (see page 14). Dried *shiitake* mushrooms have a stronger taste than fresh *shiitake* mushrooms.

Japanese horseradish (*wasabi*)

Kelp (*konbu*)

Lotus root (*renkon*)

Pickled ginger (*gari*)

Pickled radish (*takuwan*)

Fermented soybean paste (*miso*)—available in specialty food stores, it is used in soups, stocks, and dressings. *Miso* is unique to Japanese cooking and it is high in protein. The lighter (white) variety tends to be less salty than the richer red variety, and low-salt varieties are also available. Kept sealed and refrigerated, it will last for several months.

Fish cake (*kamaboko*)—puréed white fish, pressed into solid blocks and sold ready cooked. It is usually white or tinted pink and frequently used as an edible garnish. It should be stored sealed in a refrigerator.

Fish paste (*oboro*)—fine flakes of cooked and ground white fish, seasoned with sugar and occasionally colored with cochineal or red food dye. Used as a garnish or decoration for rice, it can be made at home (see page 58) or bought ready-made.

Japanese horseradish (*wasabi*)—also known as Japanese mustard and in sushi bar parlance as *namida*—"tears"—because its sharp, hot taste can cause eyes to water. *Wasabi* is an essential sushi ingredient and is made from the grated root of a riverside plant native to Japan. It is available as a paste in tubes or as a dried powder to be mixed with water. Powdered *wasabi* is better than the ready-made variety, which tends to lose its distinctive "bite" fairly quickly.

Kelp (*konbu*)—a type of dried seaweed used to make stock. It comes in the form of leathery strips, and is a prime source of iodine. Kelp should be wiped to clean it (rinsing will wash away flavor and nutrients) and not over-boiled or it will become bitter-tasting. It should be stored in an airtight container.

Lotus root (*renkon*)—white root of the water lily, sold fresh, canned, or frozen. Fresh lotus roots should be stored in a cool, dark place, and require lengthy simmering before eating.

Oba (*aojiso* or *shiso*)—also known as green perilla and Japanese basil. This aromatic jagged-edged leaf is commonly used as a garnish.

Pickled burdock root (*yama–gobo*)—long, slender root vegetable with a crunchy texture.

Pickled ginger (*gari*)—this pink or beige, pickled root ginger is eaten in small quantities between orders to clear the palate and increase the appreciation of the next dish. Fine strips of folded, pickled ginger are also used as garnish (see page 23).

Sushi rice (*sushi-meshi*)

sweet rice vinegar (*mirin*), citrus vinegar dressing (*ponzu*)

Rice vinegar (*su*), sushi vinegar (*sushi-zu*)

Rice wine (*sake*)

Seaweed (*wakame*)

Pickled radish (*takuwan*)—dried and then pickled white or giant radish (*daikon*), usually dyed yellow.

Rice (*kome*)—a matured, short-grain rice is the most suitable for sushi. (See also Sushi rice)

Rice vinegar (*su*)—very mild, clear to brown colored vinegar used to make sushi vinegar. It should always be used when available, but diluted cider vinegar may be substituted.

Rice wine (*sake*)—the national alcoholic drink of Japan and the most suitable accompaniment to sushi along with Japanese tea. In cooking, it is used in sparing amounts. A substitute for *sake* is dry sherry. The taste of *sake* ranges from sweet to dry.

Seaweed (*wakame*)—most commonly sold in dried form, often ready-shredded. Fresh *wakame* can be shredded to make a bright green garnish, or used in soups and salads after soaking for five minutes in cold water. It is highly nutritious and low in calories. *Wakame* should never be cooked for long.

Seaweed paper (*nori*)—made from chopped, dried purple laver seaweed, it is rolled into paper-thin sheets and used to wrap sushi. It rapidly loses its aroma unless kept in an airtight container or frozen. Before use, just one side of the sheet of *nori* should be lightly toasted to bring out the flavor; about 30 seconds over a gas flame is sufficient to turn it from inky black to dark green. Check before toasting, as some brands are pre-toasted. It can be used in a flaked form (*ao-nori*) as a seasoning. Cut seaweed paper with kitchen scissors or slice through it using the tip of a knife on a smooth surface.

Sesame seeds (*goma*)—used with discretion to enhance certain kinds of sushi. For the best flavor, they should be dry roasted or toasted in a hot, cast-iron pan for about one minute before they are used; keep them moving to avoid popping and burning. *Shiro goma* and *muki goma* are respectively unhulled and hulled white sesame seeds.

Shredded white radish garnish (*momiji-oroshi*)—mixture of finely shredded Japanese white radish and red chile pepper, used as a garnish (see page 24). White radish can often taste rather bitter.

Soy sauce (*shoyu*)—the best one to buy is a Japanese soy sauce (*koi kuchi shoyu*) or a sodium-reduced equivalent. Chinese dark or light soy sauce is not a good substitute.

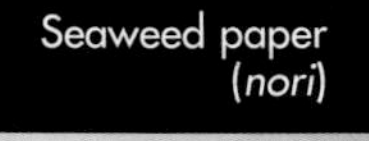
Seaweed paper (*nori*)

Soy sauce (*shoyu*)

White or giant radish (*daikon*)

Spinach (*horenso*)—commonly used ingredient in Japanese cuisine. For flavor and tenderness only young leaves should be used.

Sushi rice (*sushi-meshi* or *shari*)—short-grain rice seasoned with sushi vinegar (see page 25). Japanese or Californian rice should be used.

Sushi vinegar (*sushi-zu*)—essential for sushi rice, this clear rice vinegar is used to make sushi rice. It can be made at home (see page 25), or bought ready-made. *Sushi-zu* powder is an easy substitute.

Sweet rice wine (*mirin*)—also known as sweet *sake*, it is a cooking wine with only a trace of alcohol. This syrupy derivative of rice imparts a distinctive, sweet flavor. If *mirin* is unavailable, dissolve $\frac{1}{4}$ to $\frac{1}{3}$ cup of granulated sugar in $\frac{3}{4}$ cup of hot, dry *sake*.

White or giant radish (*daikon*)—larger and milder than the small red radish, this vegetable is known in Hindi as *mooli*. White radish is often cut into decorative shapes or finely-sliced to make "angel's hair" garnish (see page 24).

kitchen equipment

Other than a set of quality, very sharp knives (*hōchō*) —blunt ones will tear the fish and make fine-cutting impossible—the only specialized equipment needed is a bamboo rolling mat (*makisu*), a cedar-wood rice cooling tub (*hangiri*), and a wooden rice paddle (*shamoji*). While a non-metallic bowl and a wooden spoon will suffice for the authentic rice tub and paddle, there's no substitute for a proper rolling mat.

Bamboo rolling mat (*makisu*)

Knives (*hōchō*)

Wooden rice paddle (*shamoji*)

shiitake mushrooms

4 to 6 dried *shiitake* mushrooms, soaked for 15 to 20 minutes in hot water or for 30 minutes in cold water and squeezed dry, with ⅔ cup soaking liquid reserved

1 cup Premier Stock (see page 28)

1 tsp rice wine

2 Tbsp granulated sugar

1 Tbsp soy sauce

1 Tbsp sweet rice wine

Shiitake mushrooms are normally sold dried, and they are an essential flavor of Japanese cooking. They are commonly served as a side dish or ingredient in sushi. Their strong odor in dried form almost disappears when soaked. *Shiitake* mushrooms are expensive, but they last a long time and they go a long way.

preparing *shiitake* mushrooms

To reconstitute the *shiitake* mushrooms, soak in hot water for as little as 20 minutes, then remove the hard cores and stems before cooking. Soaking for 30 to 40 minutes means you can use the whole mushroom and makes for greater tenderness.

Mix the soaking liquid, Premier Stock, and rice wine in a heavy pan and bring to a boil. Add the mushrooms and reduce the heat. Simmer gently for about 3 minutes, basting the mushrooms frequently.

Add the sugar and continue to simmer for about 10 minutes by which time the liquid should have reduced by half. Add the soy sauce and cook for another 3 to 4 minutes, then add the sweet rice wine. Turn up the heat and continue cooking, shaking the pan, until the mushrooms are evenly coated with glaze.

Remove the mushrooms from the pan and use or serve immediately.

Shiitake mushrooms before soaking

Shiitake mushrooms after soaking

dried gourd *kampyō*

4 cups Premier Stock (see page 28)

1 Tbsp granulated sugar

1½ tsp soy sauce

A pinch of salt

Kampyō is made from the dried skin of a Japanese gourd and is packaged in long strips. It is a common ingredient in sushi rolls.

preparing dried gourd

To reconstitute dried gourd, wash in water with a scrubbing motion and rub with salt. Soak for one hour.

Pre-cook in a pan of boiling water for 5 to 10 minutes, and drain.

Simmer for 5 minutes in the Premier Stock, seasoned with the granulated sugar, soy sauce, and salt. Remove from the stock and lightly drain ready for use.

Dried gourd before soaking

Dried gourd after soaking

A serving of finger sushi and rolled sushi for one person.

buying and preparing fish

For sushi, absolute freshness is of the utmost importance. Ideally, the fish should be fresh-caught, and some sushi chefs will even cut slices from live fish. Some types of fatty fish and shellfish are suitable for sushi if they were frozen immediately on capture; others become too watery or discolored on thawing.

A fresh fish has bright, clear eyes with no evidence of blood, and the eyes will sit proud, not sunk into the head. The scales will be glossy and the gills bright red. When pressed with a finger, the flesh will spring back and not hold the indentation. Above all, and usually most obvious, will be the lack of a fishy smell.

If you are buying fillets, not whole fish, the meat should be firm, and the cut surface should have a sheen.

Once you have selected the fish, it should be dressed as soon as possible. You can do this yourself or ask the fishmonger to do it for you. There are two ways to fillet a fish for sushi. The first, used for most fish except flatfish, yields three fillets and a skeleton. The second method—five-piece fillet—is used for flatfish and larger fish such as bonito (see pages 18 to 21).

Dressed fish should be prepared and eaten immediately or covered with a damp cloth and refrigerated for a few hours. For an overnight stay in the refrigerator, cover the fish with plastic wrap.

Tsukiji fish market, Tokyo

Artfully arranged sushi

thawing frozen fish

Allow fish to thaw as slowly as possible, preferably overnight in a refrigerator. Soaking in water to speed up the process can result in a serious loss of flavor, but if you are in a hurry, add 2 teaspoons of salt for every 2 cups of water for freshwater fish; and for saltwater fish, add 1 tablespoon of salt for every 2 cups of water.

shellfish

Shellfish should be alive when bought, though live squid and octopus can be hard to come by. Octopus is usually boiled, and then sliced thin for sushi. A live shellfish does not float and feels heavy when picked up. The shell of a live bivalve will remain firmly closed. Shellfish will survive for some days in water stored in a refrigerator at a temperature of between 35°F and 40°F.

three-piece fillet *san-mai oroshi*

If the fish, for example sea bream, requires scaling, hold the tail of the fish firmly and scrape off the scales by pushing the knife flatly across the skin toward the head. Never hold the body of the fish as this will bruise the flesh and destroy its firmness. While de-scaling both sides, keep rinsing the fish in lightly salted water.

❶ Lay the fish on its side, and to remove the head make a diagonal cut with a sharp knife from behind the side fins, starting from the belly.

❷ Slice backward along the belly toward the anal (pelvic) fin, and remove the stomach and viscera. Clean the fish thoroughly under cold running water.

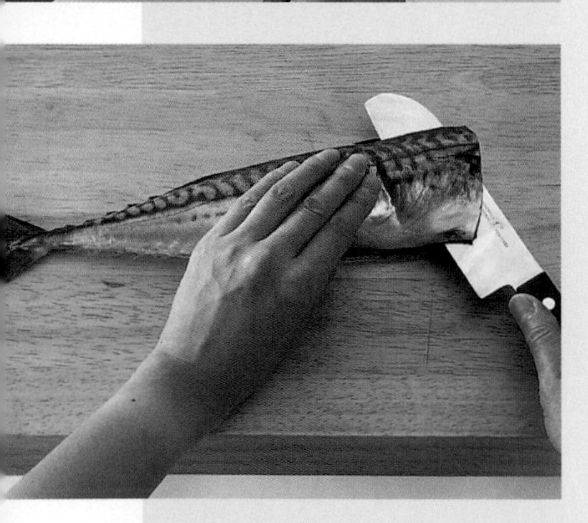

❸ Rest one hand lightly on top of the fish and cut along the back from head to tail so that the knife skims the rib cage. Carefully lift off the fillet.

❹ Lay the remaining section of fish with the skin uppermost. Rest a hand gently on the fish and slide the knife along the back between the flesh and bone from the head to the tail.

❺ Slide the knife along the belly, cutting through the base of the tail to release the second fillet. Use your fingers to gently feel the fillets for any remaining bones.

❻ The result is a fish in three pieces; a left and right fillet, and a skeleton. Large fillets can be halved along their length.

five-piece fillet *go-mai oroshi*

There are two variations of the five-piece filleting technique. One is used for flatfish, and the other for particularly large fish such as bonito. For the home sushi-maker, only the flatfish technique is relevant as fish large enough to require the five-piece filleting technique are generally too large for home consumption.

The fish shown here is brill (*karei*).

flatfish

❶ Rest one hand lightly on the head of the fish and make two deep cuts behind the gills. Turn the fish belly-up and cut through to remove the head. Squeeze out the stomach and viscera and clean the fish thoroughly under cold running water.

❷ Flip the fish over and cut through to the spine from head to tail.

❸ Keeping the knife blade flat, slide it along the bone to release the flesh.

❹ Starting from the tail, slide the knife along the outside edge of the fish to release the first fillet.

❺ Reverse the fish and follow steps 2 to 4 to remove the second fillet. Turn the fish over and repeat to remove the third and fourth fillets.

❻ The result is a fish in five pieces. The four fillets taken from near the side fins, called *engawa,* are highly-prized.

slicing a fillet

Above all else, the secret of sushi-making is to keep your hands wet. Otherwise, the fish will dry out and the rice will stick to your fingers. This was a recurrent problem throughout the photography for this book: a sushi chef (*itamae*) works fast, and slowing down means dried-out sushi. To keep your hands wet, dip them in a mixture of rice vinegar and water—about 2 tablespoons of rice wine to every 2 cups of water. Float a slice of lemon on top.

Knives are used wet, and are cleaned frequently. Either wipe the blade with a damp cloth, or dip the tip into the rice vinegar and water mixture and tap the handle on the counter, holding the knife upright, to spread the water along the blade. Wipe or rinse the knife regularly so the flavors of different ingredients do not mingle.

Always trim the fish ruthlessly—only the very finest and most tender slices are suitable for sushi or *sashimi*.

❶ Wet the knife in a bowl of water vinegar with lemon.

❷ When cutting slices of fish from a squared-off fillet, slice the end piece on the diagonal. The first piece is not suitable for *sashimi* or finger sushi, but is fine as a filling for rolled sushi. Now that one end of the fillet reveals a diagonally- or bias-cut face, cut slices from the fillet on the diagonal. Cutting on the diagonal or bias is called *sakudori*.

decorative garnishes

pickled ginger rose

Wafer-thin strips of pickled ginger can be rolled to create a "rose." One "rose" is sufficient edible garnish for a dish of sushi.

fish cake knot

❶ Slice a 1/4-inch thick piece from the fish cake. Cut a slit lengthways down the center of the slice.

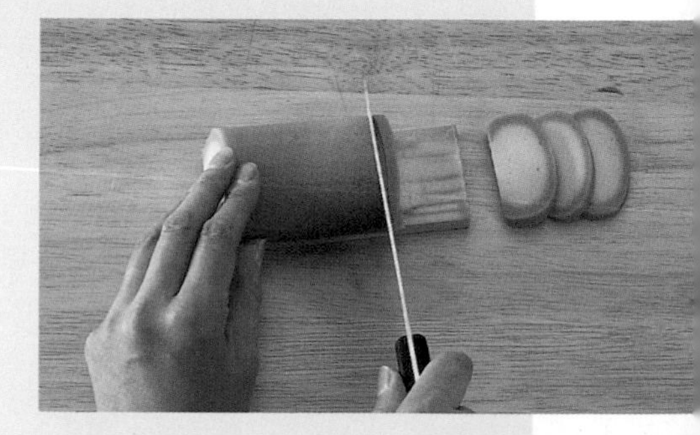

❷ Make two cuts to create ends on either side of the central cut.

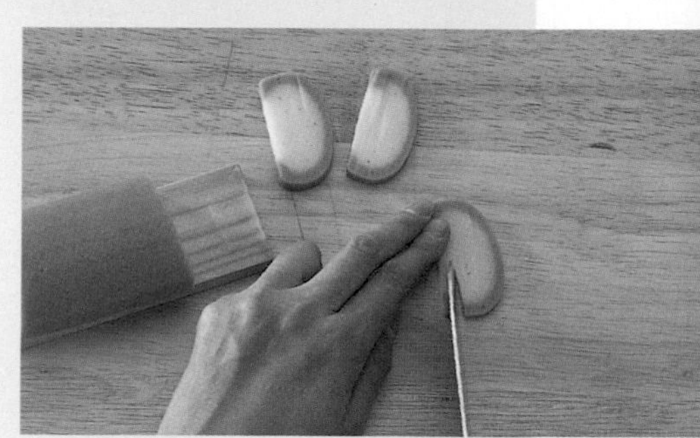

❸ Fold the ends through the central cut to create the garnish.

❹ The finished fish cake knot.

white radish "angel's hair"

❶ Peel a 2-inch long cylinder of white radish to create a fine, continuous "ribbon."

❷ Lay the "ribbon" of radish flat on a cutting surface, and cut into very fine strips. To make curly strips, cut the radish on the bias.

shredded white radish garnish (*momiji-oroshi*)

Use the pointed end of a chopstick to pierce holes in a piece of white radish. Use the chopstick to push long red chiles into the radish. Then use a grater to shred the radish finely.

cucumber pine tree

Cut a 3-inch section from the end of an unpeeled cucumber on the diagonal. Trim the end, then score the skin with parallel lines along its length. Holding the knife flat to the cucumber, slice under the skin to make the four flaps. As you slice each flap, push it to one side or the other.

Decorate with tiny roe.

sushi rice *sushi-meshi*

This is the basic technique for producing the glutinous, vinegar-flavored rice that forms the basis of all types of sushi. Matured, Japanese or Californian short-grain rice is essential. To vary the quantity of cooked rice, remember that the ratio of uncooked rice to water should be 1 part rice to 1¼ parts water.

This recipe will make one quantity of rice, which is sufficient for
2 uncut large rolls (*futomaki-zushi*)
or
4 uncut small rolls (*hosomaki-zushi*)
or
16 finger sushi (*nigiri-zushi*)

¾ cup uncooked, matured, short-grain rice

1 cup cold water

1- to 2-inch strip dried kelp, wiped clean

sushi vinegar (*sushi-zu*)

1½ Tbsp rice vinegar

1 Tbsp superfine sugar

½ tsp salt

❶ Start by washing the rice thoroughly until the water comes clear. Let the rice drain for 30 to 60 minutes to allow the grains to absorb moisture and start to swell.

❷ In a pan with a tight-fitting lid, add the rice, water, and kelp. Bring the mixture to a boil over a medium heat, removing the kelp just before boiling point. Cover the pan and simmer for about 10 minutes. (Simmering time will vary depending on the quantity of rice.) Resist the temptation to lift the lid while the rice is cooking.

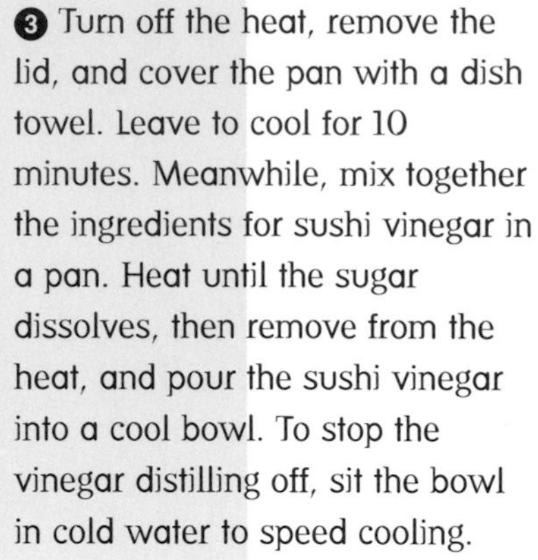

❸ Turn off the heat, remove the lid, and cover the pan with a dish towel. Leave to cool for 10 minutes. Meanwhile, mix together the ingredients for sushi vinegar in a pan. Heat until the sugar dissolves, then remove from the heat, and pour the sushi vinegar into a cool bowl. To stop the vinegar distilling off, sit the bowl in cold water to speed cooling.

❹ Using a wooden rice paddle, spoon the rice into a rice tub or bowl. Spread it out evenly, then run the paddle briefly through the rice cutting it first from side-to-side, then from top-to-bottom.

❺ Continue cutting—never mashing or stirring—the rice, adding the sushi vinegar a little at a time. At the same time, ask someone to fan the rice to cool it. It should take about 10 minutes to thoroughly mix in the sushi vinegar and bring the rice to room temperature.

soups & stocks

28 **premier stock**
dashi

28 **instant premier stock**

28 **Japanese clear soup**
suimono

28 ***miso* soup**
miso-shiru

29 **clear soup with egg and leek**
tamago no sumashi jiru

30 ***miso* soup with seaweed and onion**
wakame to tama-negi no miso-shiru

chapter 1

When it comes to the practical aspect of preparing many dishes simultaneously, remember that soups—along with noodles—are always served fresh and hot. One cup of soup is sufficient for an individual serving. Japanese soup is sipped from the bowl with any pieces of bean curd, vegetable, or seafood being eaten with chopsticks.

premier stock (*dashi*)

Premier Stock is a fundamental ingredient of much Japanese cooking. This aromatic liquid is used in preparing several kinds of cooked ingredients and for soup. Vary the quantity of dried bonito flakes to suit your palate—do not be afraid of using less than recommended here. Remove the kelp promptly or the stock will become cloudy and bitter.

makes 4 cups

6-inch strip dried kelp, cut into 3 pieces

4 cups water

½ cup dried bonito flakes

Place the kelp in a pan with the water, and bring to a boil. As soon as the water boils, remove the kelp.

Add the bonito flakes to the stock. Do not stir. When the stock returns to a boil, remove the pan from the heat. When the bonito flakes sink, the stock is ready.

Strain the stock through a fine-mesh strainer. Reserved kelp and the drained bonito flakes can be re-used to make a less strongly-flavored stock.

instant premier stock

Instant Premier Stock can be made from freeze-dried stock granules that are available from specialty food stores. To reconstitute the stock, stir 1 teaspoon of granules into 2½ cups of cold water in a pan. Bring to a boil and allow the stock to cool ready for use.

Though this is the no-fuss alternative to making the "real thing," the experts are divided about the quality of the instant stock.

Japanese clear soup (*suimono*) and *miso* soup (*miso-shiru*)

There are many kinds of soup that use Premier Stock as a base, but the ones usually encountered with sushi are *suimono* and *miso-shiru.*

Pre-cooked white fish, shellfish, chicken breast, uncooked bean curd or raw egg in combination with scallions or onions are suitable ingredients for *suimono.*

Vegetables, seaweed, mushrooms, bean curd, white fish, shellfish, chicken, or pork are commonly used ingredients in *miso-shiru.*

clear soup with egg and leek *tamago no sumashi jiru*

makes 2 cups

2¼ cups Premier Stock (see page 28)

1-inch piece of leek, halved and sliced fine

3 fresh *shiitake* mushrooms, sliced

½ tsp salt

A dash of soy sauce

1 egg, beaten

This clear soup is usually eaten with sushi dishes and has a subtle flavor. The use of *shiitake* mushrooms adds extra taste. Do not boil the leek for too long as it needs to retain some of its texture.

❶ In a pan bring the Premier Stock to a boil then add the leek, mushrooms, salt, and soy sauce. Simmer for 3 to 4 minutes.

❷ Gradually add the beaten egg to the pan, whisking continuously to stop it forming lumps. Serve immediately.

miso soup with seaweed and onion

wakame to tama-negi no miso-shiru

makes 2 cups

2¼ cups Premier Stock (see page 28)

½ medium onion, sliced

2 tsp dried *wakame* seaweed

2 Tbsp *miso* paste

This is the easiest soup you will ever make. In Japan, it is served at breakfast, lunch, or dinner, and is accompanied by a main dish and a bowl of rice. *Miso* soup varies according to the tastes of every family and each household has its favorite combinations.

❶ In a pan, bring the Premier Stock and onion to a boil. Simmer until the onion becomes transparent.
❷ Add the seaweed and continue to simmer for about 2 minutes or until it has expanded. (This only takes a couple of minutes.)
❸ Heat for a few more minutes until the soup starts to boil. Do not allow the soup to boil for more than 1 to 2 minutes or it will be too salty. Add the *miso* paste and stir using a small whisk until dissolved. Serve immediately.

finger sushi

nigiri-zushi

32 **making finger sushi**

35 **tuna, yellowtail, and bonito**
maguro, hamachi, and *katsuo*

36 **shrimp**
ebi

38 **conger eel**
anago

39 **horse-clam**
mirugai

40 **mackerel and shad**
saba and *kohada*

42 **abalone**
awabi

44 **sea bream**
tai

46 **egg pancake**
tamago

48 **halibut and salmon**
hirame and *sake*

49 **octopus**
tako

50 **squid**
ika

chapter 2

making finger sushi *nigiri-zushi*

1 quantity of sushi rice (see pages 25 to 26)

Toppings, freshly-prepared and sliced (see pages 35 to 50)

Japanese horseradish

Soy sauce and pickled ginger, to serve

Nigiri literally means "squeezing," and squeezing is the essential technique employed when making, what we have called here, finger sushi.

There are several classic shapes for the "pillow" of rice, but most usual are the elongated dome shape and the fan shape. The one shown here is the former, and the method illustrated is the one employed by master sushi chefs (*itamae*).

If you've had a chance to watch an *itamae* at work, you'll doubtless have been mesmerized by their speed and the perfectly uniform *nigiri-zushi* they create. Trying to do the same in your kitchen while chatting with friends can result in sushi that are slightly less than perfect. Learning how to pick up and roll the right amount of rice takes practice, as does knowing just how much pressure to apply.

Tuna, shrimp, salmon, squid, egg pancake, and salmon are very popular ingredients for finger sushi.

Ready yourself to prepare the finger sushi by having the tub of rice on your right side and a small amount of Japanese horseradish squeezed in a small bowl.

The step-by-step instructions are written for right-handed people; left-handed people should simply read "left hand" wherever "right hand" is used, and vice-versa.

1. With the tub of sushi rice on your right, pick up the topping with the left hand. Pick up a ball of rice about the size of a golf ball with your right hand and roll it lightly against the wall of the rice tub or bowl.

❷ With the rice ball held in the palm of your hand, dip your right index finger into the horseradish, and smear it down the center of the topping.

❸ With the topping lying flat over the fingers of the left hand, lay the rice on the topping.
Lightly press the rice with the thumb of your left hand.

❹ Hold the sushi with the thumb, while the fingers of the right hand compress the sides.

❺ Curl your left hand around the sushi, positioning the thumb near the end of the topping. Use the first two fingers of your right hand to flatten the sushi.

❻ Transfer the sushi to your right hand.

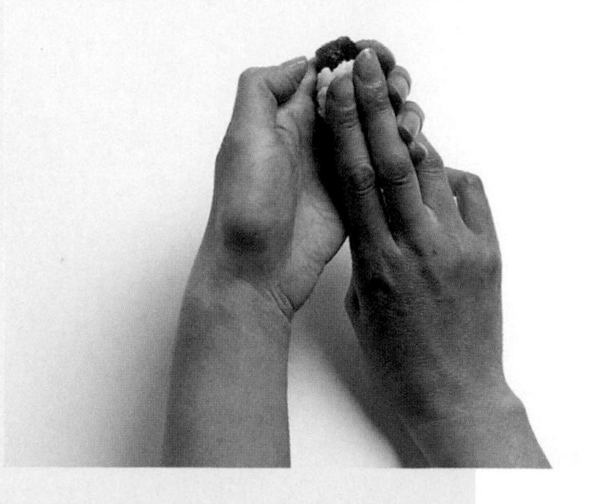

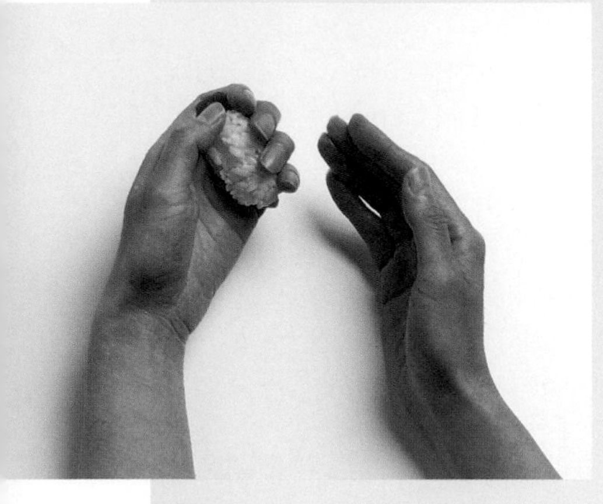

❼ Return it to the left hand so that the end held by the thumb in step 5 is nearest you.

❽ Curl your left hand around the sushi, and repeat the method shown in step 5.

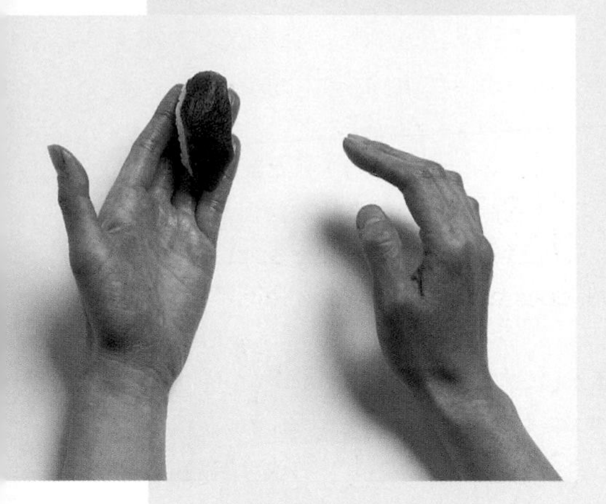

❾ Roll the sushi onto the fingers of your left hand, so that the topping is uppermost.

❿ Use the fingers of your right hand to even out the shape.

tuna, yellowtail, and bonito

maguro, hamachi, and katsuo

Tuna (*maguro*), yellowtail (*hamachi*), and bonito (*katsuo*) are classic sushi fish. Fine bias-cut slices are used for finger sushi, while less-than-perfect pieces are used in rolled sushi. Tuna and yellowtail are big fish so it is more practical and definitely easier if you buy cuts of meat, rather than the whole fish. Yellowtail can be difficult to find. Properly prepared tuna and yellowtail will have been filleted as a five-piece cut (see pages 20 to 21), with each of the side fillets cut lengthways into two blocks (*cho*). Bonito are smaller and can be bought whole.

The most expensive cut from the tuna is the lighter-colored, fatty meat (*ōtoro*) which may appear on North American sushi menus as Toro Tuna. The leaner, pinkish meat is called *chutoro*. The red meat from around the spine is known as *akami*. The cheapest, though still delicious, is the red meat cut from the strong tail muscles.

There is less variation in the meat of the yellowtail. Sushi cut from the outer meat of the fish at the top of the block (*cho*) has a strongly-flavored band or corner of dark meat (*chiai*) at the end of the slice. Sushi cut from the bottom of the block does not always have this.

preparing tuna, yellowtail, and bonito

Bonito (*katsuo*) is a variety of tuna fished from the warmer waters of the Pacific. In California, bonito, with its dark red flesh, has become very popular. Though often served raw, fillets of bonito can be lightly broiled on skewers over an open flame. The broiled meat is then rapidly cooled in ice water before being sliced for sushi. *Katsuo* may be served garnished with minced garlic or fresh ginger.

Construct the tuna, yellowtail, or bonito sushi using the sushi rice and Japanese horseradish as shown on pages 32 to 34.

Tuna *nigiri-zushi*

shrimp *ebi*

1 medium to large, fresh, uncooked shrimp per sushi

Wet bamboo skewers or metal skewers

Ice-cold water

1 quantity of sushi rice (see pages 25 to 26)

Japanese horseradish

Lemon slices and pickled ginger, to serve

Shrimp are traditionally served cooked. Only the very freshest "sweet" shrimp is served raw. The trick with cooked shrimp is to keep them straight while they are cooking, and this is done by inserting a metal or bamboo skewer into the shrimp prior to cooking.

Stainless steel skewers are the most convenient, though bamboo skewers are more traditional. If you use bamboo skewers, wet them before use. Dropping the cooked shrimp into ice-cold water will improve the color and make it easier to remove the skewer. Twist the skewer as you remove it.

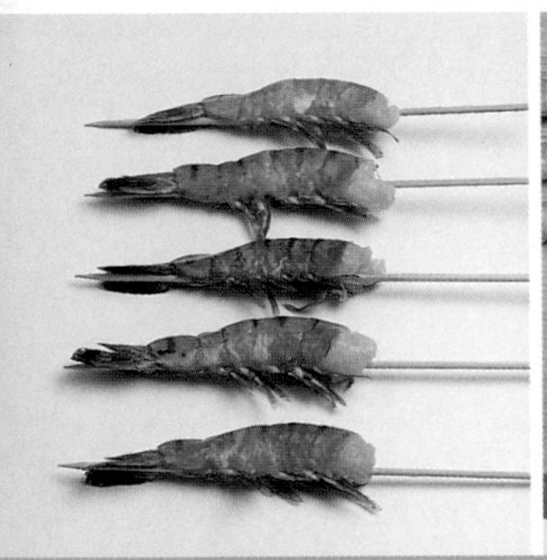

1

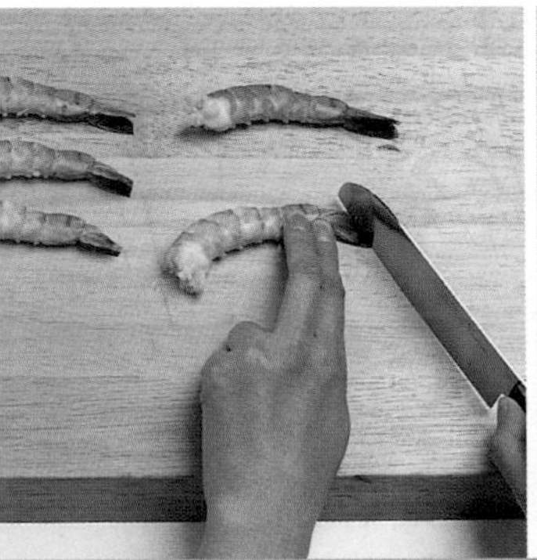

2

3

❶ Remove the head, then wash the shrimp. Remove the vein by inserting a toothpick between the joints and the shell. Skewer the shrimp. In a pan, bring water to a boil and drop in the shrimp. Remove when the shrimp rise to surface. Drop immediately into ice water and remove the skewer.
❷ Peel the shrimp, leaving the tail intact. Trim the tail at an angle to remove just the tip ends.
❸ Slice into the belly of the shrimp, but do not cut all the way through to the back.

4

❹ Open and gently flatten the shrimp in readiness to construct the sushi. Alternatively, serve it "butterfly" style by turning the shrimp inside out. Construct the shrimp sushi using the rice and Japanese horseradish as shown on pages 32 to 34. Serve with lemon and pickled ginger.

conger eel *anago*

Fresh eel is hard to obtain and its preparation can be difficult and time-consuming. For home preparation it is much easier to buy cooked conger eel (*kabayaki*) from Japanese specialty stores.

Many sushi bars have their own eel specialties, but usually the eel is filleted before being boiled in a mixture of soy sauce, rice wine, sweet rice wine, and sugar, and basted in sweet rice wine and sugar.

preparing conger eel

Construct the sushi in the conventional way, using the rice and cut pieces of eel following the method shown on pages 32 to 34, but omitting the Japanese horseradish. Bind the completed *nigiri-zushi* with strips of seaweed and sprinkle lightly with sesame seeds to serve.

horse-clam *mirugai*

Various types of clam are popular in Japan, though they are not so common in the West. The long, muscular siphon (tubular organ) of the horse-clam or geoduck (*mirugai*) is reasonably priced and relatively easy to obtain. *Mirugai* are found off the coasts of Japan and north-west America.

preparing horse-clam

Remove the siphon and pour boiling water over it to loosen the skin. Skin and thoroughly clean the siphon. As usual, cut the flesh on the bias. Tenderize the sliced flesh by hammering it with the flat of the knife blade.

Prepare the sushi following the method shown on pages 32 to 34. Clam is a slippery fish so secure the flesh to its pillow of rice with a strip of seaweed paper.

mackerel and shad

saba and *kohada*

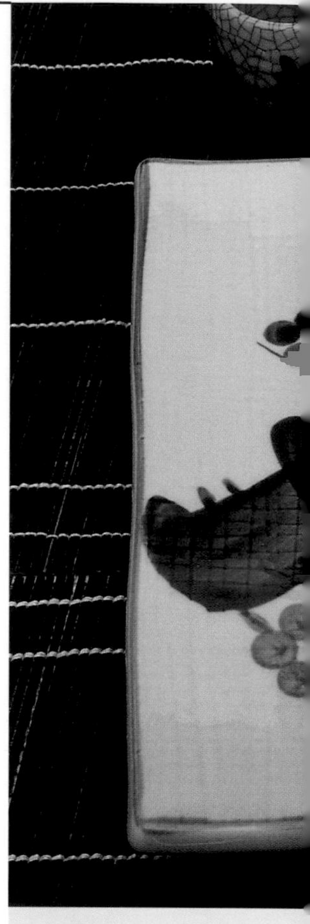

Mackerel (*saba*) and gizzard shad (*kohada*) are members of the herring family, and are prepared for finger sushi in much the same way. They are both examples of *hikari-mono*, which means "things that shine," so called because their scales have been removed leaving their shiny silvery skin intact. "Shiny" fish are usually marinated before eating to "lighten" the taste.

Should you be buying your fish from a Japanese store, the gizzard shad may be known by these names: *nakazumi, shinko,* or *konoshiro*. Each name describes the shad at a different stage of maturity.

1

2

3

❶ Carefully fillet the mackerel or shad using the three-fillet cut (see pages 18 to 19).
❷ Generously sprinkle the fillets with salt. Cover and leave the shad fillets for 1 to 2 hours, and the mackerel for upwards of 4 hours.
❸ Wash off the salt, then marinate the fillets in a mixture of 1 cup of rice vinegar and 2 tablespoons of granulated sugar. Cover and leave in the refrigerator. Allow the shad to marinate for 15 minutes, and the mackerel for 30 to 60 minutes. The marinating times can be reduced for extremely fresh fish.

Shad (left) and mackerel (right) *nigiri-zushi*

4

making the sushi

❹ Slice the larger mackerel into sushi-size strips measuring approximately 1 inch by 3 inches, and the smaller shad into 2 pieces. Slash the skin of the shad to reveal the contrast between the silvery skin and the flesh.

❺ Construct the mackerel and shad sushi using sushi rice (see pages 25 to 26) and Japanese horseradish as shown on pages 32 to 34. Garnish or serve with finely-sliced scallions and freshly minced ginger.

abalone *awabi*

Abalone is regarded as one of the great delicacies of sushi. Though once only served cooked, the Japanese have acquired a taste for raw abalone.

It is the adductor muscle—the foot the abalone uses to cling to the rocks—which is eaten, and as with any muscle, the meat is generally quite tough.

When buying abalone for sushi, choose smaller specimens for their more tender flesh. Ask your fishmonger to remove it from the shell and clean it. When abalone is very fresh, the flesh is hard to cut. As it loses its freshness, the flesh becomes softer and slightly discolored. If possible, buy from a fishmonger who keeps live abalone.

1

2

3

❶ Scrub the main body of the abalone with a brush and plenty of salt, then rinse thoroughly.
❷ Remove the dark fringe around the edge of the flesh. On a specimen over 4 inches in diameter, remove the large muscle on top of the flesh.
❸ Slice the flesh diagonally.

❹ Trim the slices slightly into finger-size sushi pieces.
❺ Construct the sushi using sushi rice (see pages 25 to 26), Japanese horseradish, and the abalone following the method shown on pages 32 to 34. Finish with a strip of seaweed paper, and serve with pickled ginger.

sea bream *tai*

The sea bream is regarded as the finest fish for sushi, and is usually served raw after being filleted using the three-fillet cut (see pages 18 to 19). If raw is not for you, then the filleted sea bream can be partially cooked by pouring boiling water over the skin. The traditional way to do this is shown below.

Other fish with firm, pale flesh that are prepared in the same way are sea bass (*suzuki*), snappers, and porgies. Grunts and croakers, two American fish, could, in theory, be prepared in the same way.

Because of its esteemed position in Japanese cuisine, cleaned and boned sea bream can also be served whole; its body cavity filled with sushi rice. Served like this, it is a spectacular centerpiece in a sushi boat or other set piece.

1

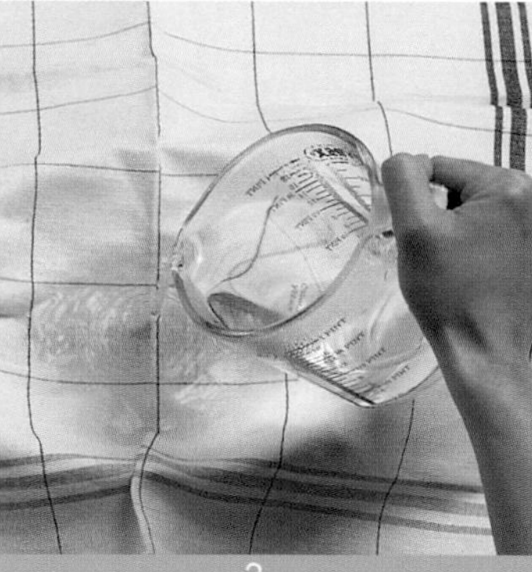

2

3

❶ Place the sea bream fillet in a shallow bowl and cover with a cloth or dish towel.

❷ Carefully pour over just-boiled water.

❸ The partially cooked fillet (right) has lost the silvery sheen to its skin, but has retained its firm, white tender flesh.

❹ Slice the filleted sea bream into strips, and construct the *nigiri-zushi* using sushi rice (see pages 25 to 26) and Japanese horseradish following the method shown on pages 32 to 34. Serve with pickled ginger and extra Japanese horseradish.

egg pancake *tamago*

makes 8 to 10 finger sushi-size slices

⅓ cup Premier Stock (see page 28)

⅓ cup granulated sugar

1½ tsp soy sauce

1½ tsp rice wine (*sake*)

½ tsp salt

5 eggs at room temperature

Vegetable oil for frying

Seaweed paper, cut into strips

Used in fine slices as a topping for finger sushi, sweetened egg pancake is also served as a side dish. While a large, rectangular omelet pan is best, the pancake can be prepared in a round one. Non-stick pans are the easiest to use. While you may like to make your first egg pancake a small one, do not reduce the quantities used here.

egg pancake mixture

Combine the stock, sugar, soy sauce, rice wine, and salt in a pan. Stir over a low heat until the sugar and salt are dissolved. Remove from the heat and allow to cool at room temperature.

In a bowl, beat the eggs, incorporating as little air as possible. Add the cooled mixture and combine with the beaten eggs.

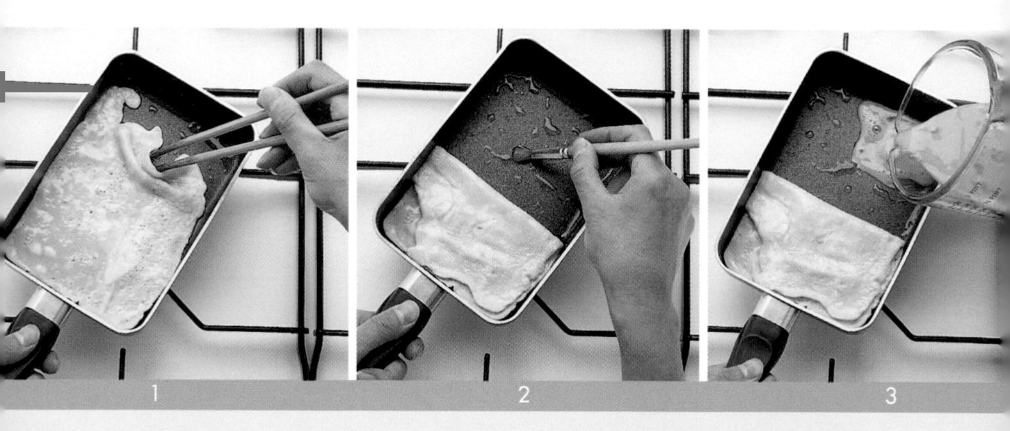

❶ Pour one quarter of the mixture into a heated, lightly-oiled pan. Tilt the pan to coat the base evenly, and cook the egg until barely set. Burst any bubbles as they form.
❷ Use a spatula or long chopsticks to fold the pancake in half and lightly oil the exposed part of the pan.
❸ Pour in one third of the remaining mixture onto the newly oiled section of the pan. Tilt the pan to spread it evenly and lift the pancake to allow uncooked mixture to run under the folded pancake. When

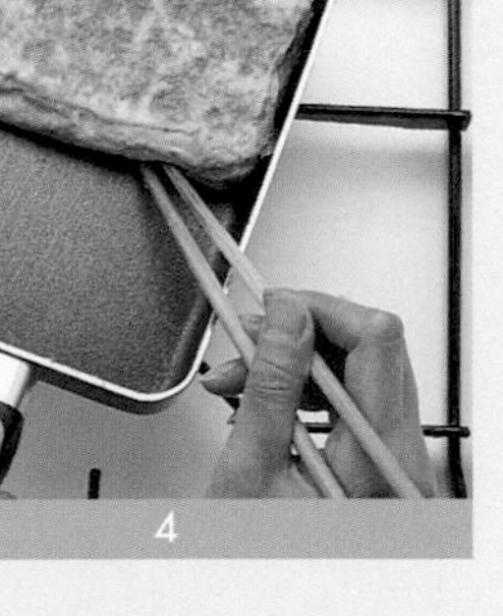
4

barely cooked, repeat the folding and oiling routine.

❹ Repeat twice more to use the remaining mixture. Finish with the pancake folded as shown. Tip out of the pan onto a smooth surface to cool before slicing into thin sushi-size strips.

❺ Construct the egg pancake finger sushi as shown on pages 32 to 34, and secure with a strip of seaweed paper. Alternatively, serve two slices of egg pancake with finely grated and drained white radish.

halibut and salmon

hirame and sake

Various types of flatfish are served as sushi, and they are all served the same way. Depending on where you live, the same or very similar fishes may be called halibut, plaice, or flounder. Flatfish sometimes appear on sushi bar menus under the unappetizing name of fluke. The prized cut from the halibut (*hirame*) is the meat near the side fins.

preparing halibut and salmon

Halibut flesh may simply be sliced and served as finger sushi with no further preparation, or it may be briefly marinated in a mixture of chopped scallions, Chinese hot pepper paste, and citrus vinegar dressing (*ponzu*).

When salmon is served as *sashimi*, the presentation is much the same as for flatfish. In Japan, salmon is not commonly served raw, but is salted to preserve it, and salted fish does not lend itself to *sashimi*. However, in California and on the East Coast, where salmon is very popular, salmon *sashimi* and *nigiri-zushi* are much in demand.

Once you've prepared the sushi following the method shown on pages 32 to 34, the sushi can be garnished with chopped scallion and shredded white radish garnish (see page 24).

Halibut (top) and salmon (bottom) *nigiri-zushi*

octopus *tako*

Octopus is always lightly cooked—never served raw—and only the tentacles are used for sushi. Though cooked, it is imperative that only the freshest and therefore most tender octopus is used.

Like shellfish, octopus past its best can cause gastric upsets, sometimes serious. For this reason buy the octopus already gutted and cleaned from a specialty store known for the freshness of its wet fish (a sushi chef would settle for nothing less than a live octopus) and the preparation skill of its staff. It is extremely hard to judge the freshness of octopus, and the only two telltale signs of a vintage specimen are pale gray, speckled skin and tentacles that bounce when shaken.

preparing fresh octopus

To cook a cleaned and fresh octopus, bring a large pan of water to a vigorous, rolling boil. Lower in the octopus slowly, tentacles first. Cook until the tentacles are red and resilient.

Cut the tentacles on the bias using a very sharp knife. A sushi chef will often wiggle the blade up and down while cutting. This makes the octopus easier to cut and produces attractive slices. Slice off the dark upper surface of the tentacle, but leave the sucker side uncut. Use a knife to score the underside of each slice. This will help it keep its place on top of the sushi rice.

Prepare the finger sushi as shown on pages 32 to 34, and finish by binding with seaweed paper. Serve with extra Japanese horseradish.

squid *ika*

Squid is a very important sushi topping, but until recently it was always cooked. Raw squid is pallid white in color and has a texture that does not appeal to everyone. Cooked squid has a purplish-red skin. Many modern sushi restaurants serve both.

Whereas the tentacles are the main attraction of octopus, it is the outer body of the squid that makes it to the sushi plate.

preparing whole, fresh squid

Liberally cover your hands with salt and grip the body in one hand and the tentacles with the other. Pull to separate the tentacles from the body. The tentacles should come away, complete with the entrails. Discard. Clean the body with plenty of salt. Pull off the fins and the thick skin and discard. Rinse and dry the body. The squid can now be sliced and served raw, or cooked.

to cook

Cut along one side of the body pouch and lay the body flat. Score the upper surface with diagonal cuts every 1/4-inch to prevent the squid curling and to give it an attractive texture. Bring a large pan of water to a vigorous, rolling boil, drop in the squid, and cook for only 15 seconds. Remove promptly, then drain and cool.

Alternatively, you may like to cook the squid in a mixture of reduced Premier Stock (see page 28), soy sauce, sweet rice wine, and granulated sugar.

Once cool, slice the squid and prepare the sushi following the method shown on pages 32 to 34.

Raw squid *nigiri-zushi* decorated with roe (top left) and plain (top right), and cooked squid bound with seaweed paper (bottom left).

rolled sushi

maki-zushi

52 **making rolled sushi**
maki-zushi

55 **small gourd rolls**
kampyō-maki

56 **small pickled radish rolls**
takuwan-maki

56 **small cucumber rolls**
kappa-maki

58 **large sushi rolls with fish paste**
futo-maki

60 **inside-out California rolls**

62 **inside-out smoked salmon rolls**

64 **rainbow rolls**

66 **small spicy tuna rolls**

chapter 3

making rolled sushi *maki-zushi*

1 quantity of sushi rice (see pages 25 to 26)

Fillings, freshly prepared and sliced (see pages 55 to 56)

Japanese horseradish

Soy sauce and pickled ginger, to serve

Any sushi that is created with the use of a bamboo rolling mat is a *maki-zushi*. It does not matter how the sushi rice, seaweed paper, and other ingredients are arranged, nor does the size matter. As we mentioned in the Introduction, small sushi rolls containing one or two ingredients are call *hoso-maki*. Larger rolls with three or more fillings are *futo-maki*.

Rolled sushi can contain almost anything, but typical ingredients include boiled spinach, carrot, cucumber, cooked dried gourd, sliced *shiitake* mushrooms, egg pancake, bamboo shoots, burdock root, fish paste, and seafood.

Whether it is because rolled sushi is easier to pick up and eat or because its flavors, textures, and colors are so appealing, *maki* is often the first Japanese dish that non-Japanese try. And because of this, chefs around the world—and in Japan—are always trying out new combinations of ingredients and ways of presenting *maki*. The result of one chef's artistry and imagination is shown in the Rainbow Rolls on page 64.

Rolled sushi, like all other sushi, should be served immediately. You can store it in the fridge for up to one hour, but doing so will result in the rice hardening and the fish losing its freshness. After 3 to 4 hours, the rice will be unpleasantly hard.

Be prepared to make these tightly-rolled sushi by having ready a quantity of sushi rice (see pages 25 to 26); sheets of seaweed paper; freshly and finely-sliced vegetables, fish, and egg pancake; and sesame seeds and Japanese horseradish. Also have on hand a bamboo rolling mat, a sharp knife, and a small bowl containing rice vinegar-water (see page 22).

❶ Cut a sheet of seaweed paper in half and place it onto the bamboo mat. Top the seaweed paper with a layer of sushi rice about ⅜-inch thick, leaving one long edge of the seaweed paper uncovered.

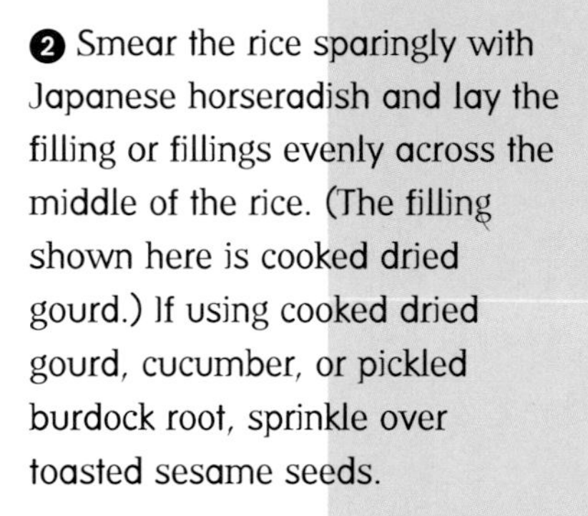

❷ Smear the rice sparingly with Japanese horseradish and lay the filling or fillings evenly across the middle of the rice. (The filling shown here is cooked dried gourd.) If using cooked dried gourd, cucumber, or pickled burdock root, sprinkle over toasted sesame seeds.

❸ Start rolling the mat from the edge nearest you. Use your fingers to hold the fillings in place. Roll as tightly and as evenly as possible without forcing the rice or fillings to ooze from the sides. The moisture from the rice helps bind and seal the seaweed paper.

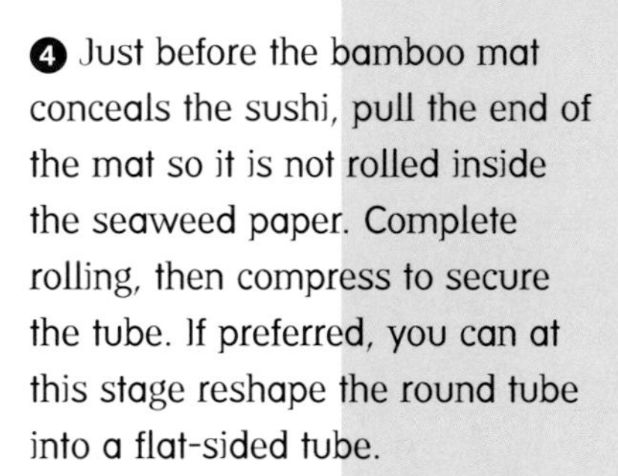

❹ Just before the bamboo mat conceals the sushi, pull the end of the mat so it is not rolled inside the seaweed paper. Complete rolling, then compress to secure the tube. If preferred, you can at this stage reshape the round tube into a flat-sided tube.

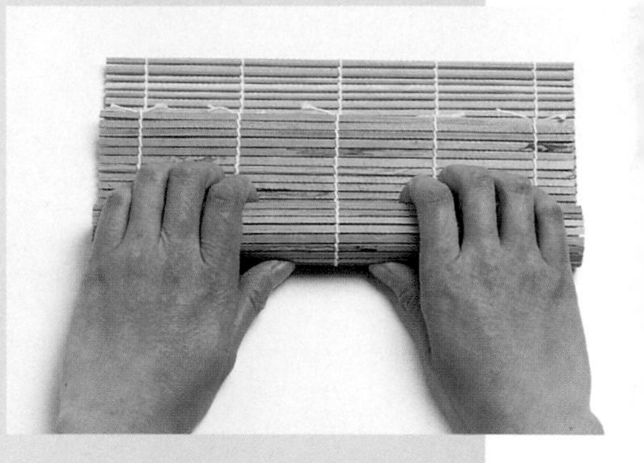

❺ Carefully pull back the mat to reveal the rolled sushi. Push in the ends if they are untidy.

❻ Dip the tip of a sharp knife into the rice vinegar-water, hold the knife point up and tap the butt so that the liquid runs down the blade. Repeat this as often as necessary when cutting.

❼ Place the roll on a cutting surface and cut in half. To cut through fillings like carrot or dried gourd, cut the rolled sushi with a steady, slicing motion and when you feel resistance, hit the back of the blade smartly with your hand to complete the cut.

❽ Lay the two halves side-by-side, and cut into thirds. The finished rolled sushi are served so that the fillings are visible.

small gourd rolls *kampyō-maki*

The shelves of Japanese foodshops are lined with unfamiliar dried foods: dried mushrooms, seaweeds, and multi-colored varieties of stringy and papery substances. Dried foods are an important part of Japanese cookery and may be easily obtained in the West, making it possible to reproduce authentic Japanese tastes. Some of the most fundamental flavors and textures of Japanese cookery are derived from dehydrated vegetables.

Kampyō also translates as calabash, and small rolls made with this traditional ingredient are very popular in Japan.

preparing gourd rolls

Follow the instructions on page 15 to reconstitute the gourd, then construct these rolls following the method shown on pages 52 to 54. Serve the gourd rolls garnished with *oba* (see page 11).

small pickled radish rolls and small cucumber rolls

takuwan-maki and kappa-maki

makes 4 rolls (*maki*), or 24 "pieces"

2 sheets seaweed paper, halved

1 quantity sushi rice (see pages 25 to 26)

Japanese horseradish

1 pickled Japanese radish, cut into ¼-sq. inch by 7½-inch long strips

1 cucumber, cut into Two ¼-sq. inch by 7½-inch long strips

2 tsp toasted sesame seeds

Rice vinegar water and slice of lemon in a bowl (see page 22)

These small sushi rolls are often referred to as "family sushi" because they are a staple of Japanese home cooking.

1

2

❶ Place one piece of seaweed paper on the bamboo mat and top with sushi rice. Spread it to a thickness of ⅜ inch and leave the long sides of the seaweed paper uncovered. For the cucumber rolls use the tip of a finger to smear a small amount of horseradish onto the rice.

❷ Place one strip of pickled radish onto the rice and sprinkle with ½ teaspoon of toasted sesame seeds.

3 4 5

❸ Start rolling the mat, applying pressure evenly and firmly.
❹ Just before the mat totally conceals the sushi, pull out the end of the mat so that it is not rolled into the sushi, complete rolling, then compress the mat to secure the seaweed paper and fillings.
❺ Unroll the mat carefully and transfer the roll to a smooth surface. Repeat to make three more pickled radish or cucumber rolls. Cut the rolls following the method shown on page 54 and arrange as pictured above. Serve with pickled ginger.

large sushi rolls with fish paste *futo-maki*

makes 2 rolls (*maki*), or 12 "pieces"

oboro

7 oz uncooked, small white-fleshed fish, cleaned, scaled, and head removed

Cochineal or red food dye

1 Tbsp granulated sugar

1 Tbsp rice wine

Salt

Oboro is a type of fish paste that has been colored with cochineal or red food dye. You can make your own *oboro* or buy it ready-made in specialty stores.

making *oboro*

In a pan, boil the fish in water until thoroughly cooked. Remove from the pan and allow to cool before removing skin and bones. Dry the fish by folding in a cloth and squeezing gently.

Pound the fish in a mortar and pestle, adding a few drops of cochineal or red food dye to tint the fish pink.

Transfer the ground fish to a heavy pan with the remaining ingredients. Cook over a moderate heat, stirring constantly until the liquid has evaporated.

Set aside to cool until required.

1

2

3

❶ Lay a sheet of seaweed paper onto the mat. Spread rice over the seaweed paper to a thickness of 3/8 inch, leaving a little of the seaweed paper exposed. Lay spinach across the rice.

❷ Add the fish paste and egg pancake and finish with the cooked dried gourd laid over the rice.

❸ Start rolling the mat from the edge nearest you. Use your fingers to hold the fillings in place. Roll as tightly and as evenly as possible, and tuck the bare ends of the seaweed paper into the body of the roll.

large sushi rolls

2 whole sheets of seaweed paper

1 quantity sushi rice (see pages 25 to 26)

4 oz spinach, boiled and well-drained

Two 8-inch strips egg pancake (see pages 46 to 47)

6 Tbsp *oboro*

Eight 8-inch strips cooked dried gourd (see page 15)

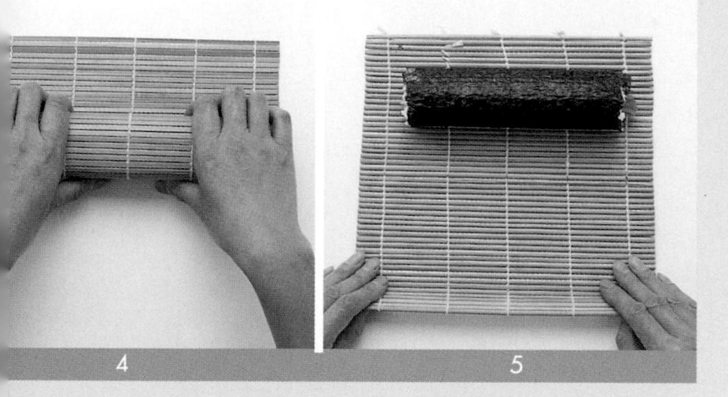

4 5

❹ Compress the roll with the bamboo mat, pressing in the ends. You can re-shape the roll to be flat-sided or slightly oval.
❺ Unroll the mat and remove the *futo-maki* onto a smooth surface. Cut it in half, then lay the pieces side-by-side, and cut in thirds again to serve. Repeat to make a second *futo-maki*.

inside-out California rolls

makes 3 rolls or 18 "pieces"

Plastic wrap

3 half-size sheets of seaweed paper

1 quantity of sushi rice (see pages 25 to 26)

Japanese horseradish

Fine-sliced cucumber

Flesh of 1 avocado

5 oz crab meat

Toasted sesame seeds and roe (optional), to garnish

As its name suggests, California Roll is hardly a classical sushi recipe. It is, however, extremely popular across the United States. It is a superb blend of textures—cooked crab, avocado, and cucumber.

Although it is quite possible to make a small roll with sparing amounts of these fillings, inside-out rolls allow for generous servings. A vegetarian version of the California Roll can be made using a combination of cucumber, cooked dried gourd (see page 15), finely-sliced parboiled carrot, snow peas, and cream cheese!

To prepare the avocado, halve it, cutting around the pit. Remove the pit and using a large spoon scoop out the flesh from each half in one piece. Slice into strips.

1

2

3

❶ Cover the sushi mat with the plastic wrap. Lay the seaweed paper on top and cover with a thin layer of sushi rice. Dip your fingers in a bowl of rice vinegar-water (see page 22), then lightly press the rice with your fingers to secure it to the seaweed.
❷ Turn the seaweed paper and rice over on the covered mat. Smear the seaweed paper with a little Japanese horseradish.
❸ Top with cucumber, avocado, and crab meat.

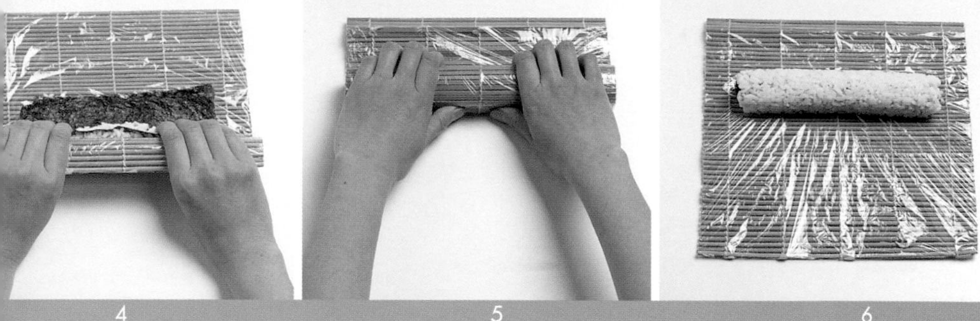

4 5 6

❹ Carefully start to roll the mat, using your fingers and palms to keep the mat even and the ingredients in place.
❺ Compress and shape the roll.
❻ Unroll the mat and remove the plastic wrap, then sprinkle with sesame seeds and roe before cutting into six pieces. Repeat to make 2 more rolls.

inside-out smoked salmon rolls

makes 3 rolls, or 18 "pieces"

Plastic wrap

3 half-size sheets of seaweed paper

1 quantity of sushi rice (see pages 25 to 26)

2-inch piece of cucumber, seeded and cut into thin strips

2 scallions, cut into thin strips

6 strips of smoked salmon, or salmon pâté, cut into ¼-sq. inch by 8-inch long strips

3 oz cream cheese, cut into thin strips

Scallions and sesame seeds, to garnish

Smoked salmon and cream cheese are not traditional Japanese ingredients. Smoked salmon, for example, is known in Japan only by its English name. But like so many other non-traditional ingredients, smoked salmon and cream cheese have become a part of the sushi culture. These rolls are an excellent way to serve sushi to people who do not like, cannot eat, or are afraid of raw fish. Use fine, translucent, slow-smoked salmon—Scottish or Canadian is best. The other name for this inside-out roll is a Kosher Roll.

❶ Cover the sushi mat with the plastic wrap. Lay the seaweed paper on top and cover with a ⅜-inch layer of sushi rice. Moisten your fingers with rice vinegar water (see page 22) and use them to lightly press the rice to secure it to the seaweed.

❷ Turn so the seaweed is uppermost. Lay a few strips of cucumber and scallions across the seaweed paper and rice.

❸ Top with generous quantities of smoked salmon so its delicate taste is not overwhelmed by the other ingredients.

❹ Lay the cream cheese alongside the smoked salmon. The filling should be closest to the roller's hands when the sushi is rolled (the roller would start rolling from the end of the mat which is uppermost in this picture). Carefully start to roll the maki, using your fingers and palms to keep it even and the ingredients in place.

❺ Unroll the mat and remove the plastic wrap. Cut the roll in half, then put the halves side-by-side and cut into thirds.

❻ Repeat to make two more rolls and serve sprinkled with fine-chopped scallions and sesame seeds.

rainbow rolls

This roll is the most colorful of the inside-out rolls. The only easy way to make them is with the aid of plastic wrap. Before the advent of plastic wrap, they were made using a cloth or a wet bamboo rolling mat.

The technique and ingredients are the same as for the California Roll (see pages 60 to 61), but fine-cut strips of fish and avocado straddle the top. Choose two fish that have different colored flesh—try white halibut or creamy yellowtail with orange smoked salmon or red bonito.

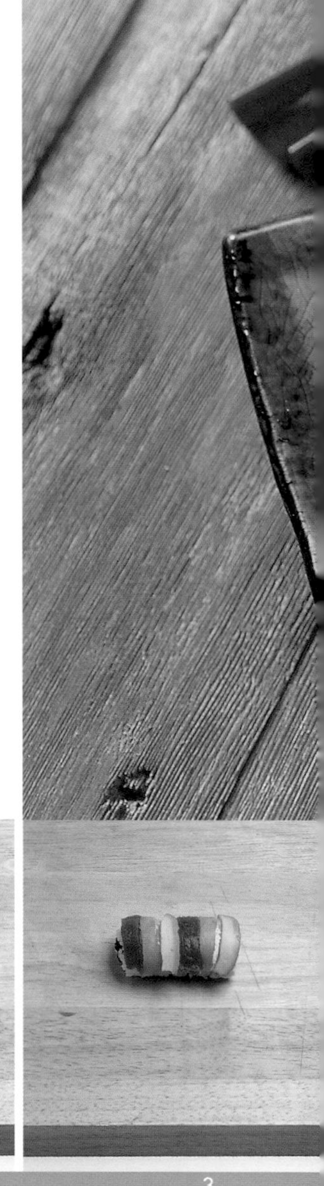

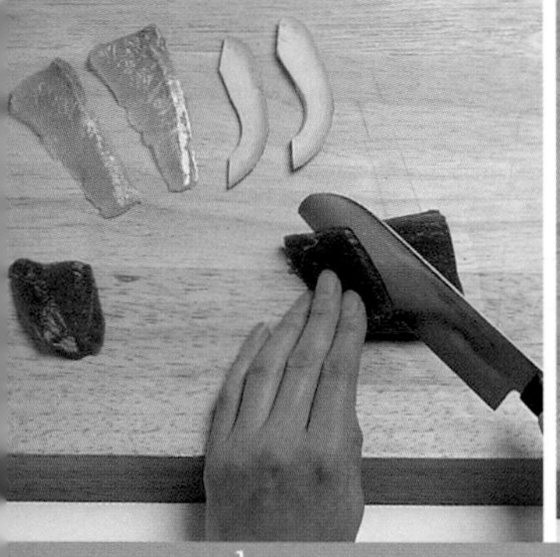

1

2

3

❶ Follow steps 1 to 5 on pages 60 to 61 to make the Inside-out California Roll. Slice the fish and avocado for the topping very thinly.
❷ Unroll the mat, remove the plastic wrap and place the California Roll on a smooth surface. Lay a strip of fish and a strip of avocado across the top of the roll.
❸ Continue laying on strips of avocado and fish, alternating the colors for maximum effect.

4

❹ Cover the roll with plastic wrap. Carefully pick up the roll using the bamboo mat. Wrap the mat tightly around the roll and compress it to even the shape and secure the slices of fish and avocado. Remove the plastic wrap and cut the roll into two or three pieces. Trim the ends to neaten and serve garnished with *oba* (see page 11).

small spicy tuna rolls

Traditionally, Japanese horseradish and vinegar were the only spices used in sushi. In the last few years, however, a new kind of spicy sushi has become increasingly popular. It is usual to make spicy sushi in the form of rolled sushi rather than finger sushi, where a marinade could easily burn the lips or tongue. In a rolled sushi, the flavors mingle before the spices hit the taste-buds.

The main "spices" used are Chinese hot pepper paste, scallions, and radish sprouts. Unless you are a lover of very "hot" foods, however, you should use them sparingly.

spicy marinade

The perfect marinade for tuna or bonito consists of 2 tablespoons of soy sauce mixed with ½ teaspoon of Chinese hot pepper paste. Pour the marinade over the slices of tuna, and top with a tiny amount of finely-chopped scallion. Allow the tuna to marinate for one hour, covered, in a cool place. Drain the tuna well to remove excess marinade before using as a filling. Make the spicy tuna rolls following the method shown on pages 52 to 54.

fancy sushi

68 **hand-rolled sushi**
temaki-zushi

70 **salmon skin rolls**
temaki-zushi

72 **roe boat sushi**
gunkan-maki

74 **scallop boat sushi and oysters**
gunkan-maki and *kaki*

75 **scattered sushi**
chirashi-zushi

76 **deep-fried bean curd pockets**
inari-zushi

chapter 4

hand-rolled sushi

temaki-zushi

Like a number of other things in this book, hand-rolled sushi are a relatively recent innovation.

"Roll your own" sushi lends itself admirably to a dinner party or buffet. Halved sheets of seaweed paper are fine for a sit-down dinner, but for a buffet a quarter of a sheet is easier to handle. As a substitute for seaweed paper, try iceberg or romaine lettuce.

Ideas for fillings—broiled chicken breasts, pâté, rare or raw beef, fish roe, shrimp, smoked salmon, fresh or canned tuna, seafood sticks, egg pancake, avocado, cooked dried gourd, carrots, watercress, cucumber, scallions, pickled ginger, boiled spinach, radish sprouts, Japanese horseradish, Chinese hot-pepper paste, and cream cheese.

Makes 8 large or 16 small *temaki*

Egg pancake (see pages 46 to 47), sliced

1½-inch piece of cucumber, cut on the diagonal into 6 rounds, and then into matchsticks

½ avocado, sliced

1 to 2 rollmop herrings, sliced

Bunch of watercress

3½ oz canned tuna in brine

1 Tbsp mayonnaise

Soy sauce

Japanese horseradish

1 quantity sushi rice (see pages 25 to 26)

4 sheets of seaweed paper, cut into quarters or halves

Arrange the egg pancake, cucumber, avocado, rollmop herring, and mustard cress on a large serving plate. Drain the tuna and mix with the mayonnaise, and spoon onto the serving plate.

Pour soy sauce and spoon Japanese horseradish into individual bowls, and serve the sushi rice and seaweed paper separately.

To eat: guests spread about 1 tablespoon of rice evenly over a piece of seaweed paper and smear on a little Japanese horseradish. They then lay a combination of two to three fillings across the middle. Carefully roll the seaweed paper into a cornet shape, and dip it into the soy sauce.

salmon skin rolls *temaki-zushi*

makes 8 rolls (*temaki*)

2 to 3 uncooked salmon fillets, skin intact

1½-inch piece of cucumber, cut on the diagonal into 6 rounds and then into matchsticks

Bunch of watercress

2 Tbsp bonito flakes

Japanese horseradish

Pickled ginger

Oba (see page 11)

1 quantity of sushi rice (see pages 25 to 26)

8 half-size sheets seaweed paper

This salmon-based *temaki* and other sushi where Western ingredients have been substituted for more traditional Japanese ingredients, are collectively called *yoshoku-zushi*, which broadly means Western-style sushi. The essential flavor of this sushi comes from the fillets of salmon that are broiled with the skin intact.

Try canned salmon mixed with mayonnaise and served with watercress as an easy alternative.

Unlike rolled sushi when compactness is a sign of a well-made *maki*, *temaki-zushi* should only be loosely rolled into a cone. Never roll *temaki-zushi* in advance or the seaweed paper will become soggy—always follow the "roll and eat, roll and eat" rule.

1

2

3

❶ Broil the salmon, skin-side up, until the fish is cooked and the skin just crisp.

❷ Allow the salmon to cool before cutting into slices. Arrange the salmon, cucumber, watercress, and bonito flakes on a large serving plate. Spoon Japanese horseradish into four small individual bowls, and serve the pickled ginger, *oba*, rice, and seaweed paper separately.

4

❸ Each guest tops the seaweed paper with a heaped tablespoon of rice and smears a little Japanese horseradish onto the rice. They then lay salmon, cucumber, watercress, and bonito flakes onto the rice.
❹ The finished *temaki* is rolled to form a cone. Serve garnished with pickled ginger and *oba*.

roe boat sushi *gunkan-maki*

Gunkan-maki which translates as "battleship roll" describes the shape of sushi used to "carry" soft fillings. One such soft filling is fish eggs or roe.

One of the most common varieties of roe is large, golden-red salmon roe (*ikura*). This is sold ready-packed, like caviar, and is one of the largest of roes. Other types include: small, red-brown, salted cod roe (*tarako*); yellow, salted herring roe (*kazu-no-ko*); lumpfish roe; and the expensive, sturgeon caviar. *Komochi konbu* is kelp on which herring have spawned. A strip of this kelp, laden with roe, can be placed atop a finger of sushi.

Salted herring roe (*kazu-no-ko*) are desalted by soaking in water for at least two hours before use.

1 2

❶ Cut seaweed paper into strips about 5 inches by 1½ inches. Lay the strip across your left hand, and use your right to pick up a ball of sushi rice (see pages 25 to 26). Roll the ball around the rice tub to form the sausage-shape. Place the rice into the middle of the seaweed paper.
❷ Roll the seaweed paper around the rice so that it is slightly skewed. This is not just to appeal to the Japanese love of asymmetry; it makes the roll easier to build.

3 4

❸ Fold the protruding edge of the seaweed paper to the underside of the "boat" and press it onto the rice.
❹ Stand the *gunkan-maki* on a smooth surface and fill with salmon roe. Serve garnished with a little Japanese horseradish and a fan of cucumber slices.

scallop boat sushi and oysters *gunkan-maki and kaki*

A swimming scallop (*hotate-gai*) is a remarkable sight. Instead of remaining peacefully on the sea floor, this bivalve opens and closes its shell to zip through the water. The adductor muscle that enables this movement is appropriately large, and it is this muscle that is used in sushi. As with the abalone, the rest of the *hotate-gai* is edible, but is not normally used in sushi.

Oyster on the half shell (left) and scallop boat sushi (right)

preparing scallops and oysters

Most sushi bars normally use frozen scallops, with smaller ones being cut into dice and served in "battleship" sushi. The larger specimens are prepared as finger sushi.

The muscle is ivory-white in color and sits in the middle of the shell, surrounded by the rest of the shellfish. Like many shellfish, scallop is most tender when raw, becoming increasingly tough with cooking. Five minutes' cooking can reduce the most tender scallop to the consistency of rubber, so care should be taken.

While oysters (*kaki*) are usually served in their open half-shell, they can be served in a boat of seaweed paper and sushi rice. Leave small oysters whole, but chop large specimens into dice.

Prepare scallop or oyster *gunkan-maki* as shown on pages 72 to 73, and garnish with a small amount of roe, finely-chopped scallions, *oba* (see page 11), shredded white radish garnish (see page 24), or even mayonnaise for a modern touch.

scattered sushi *chirashi-zushi*

This scattered sushi is the *Kanto-fu chirashi-zushi.* Kanto is in the eastern part of Japan, and it is where this dish originated. *Chirashi-zushi* consists of a bed of sushi rice (2 quantities of sushi rice serve 3), on which various kinds of fish and vegetables are arranged. Standard inclusions in this type of scattered sushi are egg pancake, cooked dried gourd, and *shiitake* mushrooms.

preparing scattered sushi

Choose from among these other ingredients for your scattered sushi: bamboo shoots, sticks of cream cheese, seaweed sheets cut into strips, radish sprouts, sheets of deep-fried bean curd cut into strips, diagonally-sliced cucumbers, green beans, Japanese horseradish, canned lotus root (first soaked for 10 minutes in rice vinegar and water), pickled ginger, seasoned *shiitake* mushrooms, boiled spinach, cucumber, egg pancake, abalone, rare or raw beef, broiled chicken, bonito, crab, eel, fish cake, seafood sticks, sea bream, shad, shrimp, smoked salmon, squid, tuna, and yellowtail.

Like "roll your own" sushi (*temaki-zushi*), *chirashi-zushi* is always a big hit at dinner parties. Serve it with soups and a selection of side dishes—salads or dishes of lightly-simmered vegetables are usually good accompaniments.

Because there are so many ways of making it, just keep experimenting until you find the mixture that suits you best.

deep-fried bean curd pockets *inari-zushi*

makes 8 bean curd pouches (*inari-zushi*)

4 bean curd pouches, halved

1 quantity of sushi rice (see pages 25 to 26)

Toasted sesame seeds

Pickled ginger

braising stock

1 cup Premier Stock (see page 28)

3 Tbsp granulated sugar

3 Tbsp soy sauce

1 Tbsp sweet rice wine

Bean curd pouches (*abura-age*)—frozen or refrigerated—are bought already deep-fried from Japanese or specialty food stores. Preparation at home includes braising in stock before stuffing with sushi rice, and sesame seeds or pickled ginger. *Inari* are an acquired taste, not because they are strongly flavored but because they are somewhat bland.

Once braised and prepared, deep-fried bean curd pockets keep well, but unfrozen ones should always be used within one day of purchase.

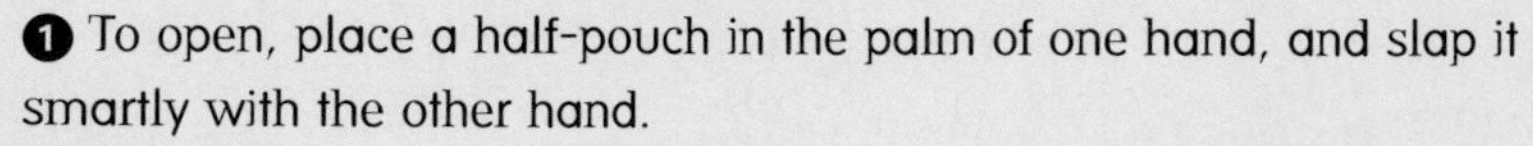

❶ To open, place a half-pouch in the palm of one hand, and slap it smartly with the other hand.
❷ Loosen the middle and prise open to create a deep pocket.

❸ Fill with sushi rice and compress the rice with a thumb. Sprinkle in sesame seeds or slivers of pickled ginger.
❹ To serve, turn the filled pouch upside-down and tuck the flaps under and press them into the rice. Serve garnished with pickled ginger.

glossary

abura-age	deep-fried bean curd
age-mono	deep-frying food
akami	dark meat from the middle of a fish
anago	conger eel
ao-nori	dried seaweed flakes
awabi	abalone
buri	yellowtail kingfish
chiai	dark outer meat of a fish
chirashi-zushi	scattered sushi
cho	side fillets of fish cut lengthwise into blocks
daikon	Japanese radish, sometimes called giant white or *mooli* radish
dashi	soup stock
ebi	shrimp or lobster
engawa	meat next to the fins on a flatfish
futo-maki	large sushi roll
gari	pickled ginger
goma	sesame seeds
go-mai oroshi	five-fillet cut for fish
gomoku-zushi	form of *chirashi-zushi*
gunkan-maki	"battleship" sushi
hako-zushi	boxed or pressed sushi
hamachi	(young) yellowtail
hangiri	rice tub for sushi rice
hikari-mono	"things that shine," referring to shiny-skinned fish
hirame	halibut
hōchō	knives
horenso	spinach
hoso-maki	small sushi rolls
hotate-gai	scallops
ika	squid (calamari)
ikura	salmon roe
inari-zushi	stuffed, deep-fried bean curd pouch
itamae	sushi chef
kabayaki	cooked conger eel
kaki	oysters
kamaboko	fish cake
kampyō	dried gourd
kani	crab
kappa-maki	small sushi roll filled with cucumber
karei	brill
katsuo	bonito (bonita)
katsuo-bushi	dried bonito flakes
kazu-no-ko	salted herring roe
kohada	gizzard shad
kome	matured, short-grain rice
konbu	type of seaweed, kelp
konoshiro	gizzard shad
maguro	bluefin tuna

maki	rolled sushi
makisu	bamboo rolling mat
mirin	sweet rice wine used in cooking
mirugai	horse-clam
miso	fermented soy bean paste
miso-shiru	type of soup
momiji-oroshi	finely shredded white radish with chile
mushi-zushi	steamed sushi
naname wa-giri	slicing diagonally
nare-zushi	fermented sushi
nigiri-zushi	squeezed or pressed sushi (finger sushi)
ninjin	carrot
nori	seaweed paper
oba	green perilla or Japanese basil
ocha	green tea
o-hashi	chopsticks
ponzu	citrus vinegar dressing
renkon	lotus root
saba	mackerel
sake	rice wine
sake	salmon
sakudori	way of cutting fish
san-mai oroshi	three-fillet cut for fish
sashimi	raw fish, served without rice
shamoji	rice paddle
sengiri	slicing an ingredient into matchsticks
shiitake	type of mushroom
shoyu	soy sauce
shoga	alternative for pickled ginger
su	rice vinegar
suimono	clear Japanese soup
sushi-meshi	sushi rice
sushi-zu	spiced, sweetened vinegar
tai	sea bream
takenoko	bamboo shoots
tako	octopus
takuwan	pickled radish
tamago	egg pancake
tarako	cod roe
temaki	hand-rolled sushi
tofu	bean curd
tsu	knowledgeable sushi-lover
unagi	freshwater eel
wakame	type of seaweed
wakegi	scallions
wasabi	Japanese horseradish, also called Japanese mustard
yaki-mono	broiling food
yama-gobo	pickled burdock root

index

a
Abalone Finger Sushi 42

b
Bean Curd Pockets, Deep-fried 76
Bonito Finger Sushi 35

c
California Rolls, Inside-out 60
Clear Soup with Egg and Leek 29
Conger Eel Finger Sushi 38
cucumber pine tree garnish 24
Cucumber Rolls 56

d
Deep-fried Bean Curd Pockets 76
dried gourd, to prepare 15

e
Egg Pancake Finger Sushi 46
egg pancake, to prepare 46

f
finger sushi, to prepare 32–4
fillet, five-piece 20–1
fillet, three-piece 18–19
fish cake knot garnish 23
Fish Paste, Large Sushi Rolls with 58
fish paste, to prepare 58
fish, to prepare 18–22
fish for sushi 16–17

g
garnishes 23–4
ginger: pickled ginger rose garnish 23
Gourd Rolls, Small 55
gourd, dried, to prepare 15

h
Halibut Finger Sushi 48
hand-rolled sushi, to prepare 68
Horse-clam Finger Sushi 39

i
Inside-out California Rolls 60
Inside-out Smoked Salmon Rolls 62
Instant Premier Stock 28

j
Japanese Clear Soup 28

l
Large Sushi Rolls with Fish Paste 58

m
Mackerel Finger Sushi 40
marinade, spicy 66
Miso Soup with Seaweed and Onion 30

o
Octopus Finger Sushi 49
Oyster Boat Sushi 74

p
pickled ginger rose garnish 23
Pickled Radish Rolls 56
Premier Stock 28
  Instant 28

r
radish: Pickled Radish Rolls 56
  white radish "angel's hair" garnish 24
  shredded white radish garnish 24
Rainbow Rolls 64
rice, sushi 25–6
Roe Boat Sushi 72
rolled sushi, to prepare 52–4

s
Salmon Finger Sushi 48
Salmon Skin Rolls 70
Scallop Boat Sushi 74
scattered sushi, to prepare 75
Sea Bream Finger Sushi 44
Shad Finger Sushi 40
shellfish for sushi 17
shiitake mushrooms, to prepare 14
shredded white radish garnish 24
Shrimp Finger Sushi 36
Small Gourd Rolls 55
Smoked Salmon Rolls, Inside-out 62
spicy marinade 66
Spicy Tuna Rolls 66
Squid Finger Sushi 50
sushi: equipment for 13
  and health 7–8
  ingredients for 10–13
  to serve 7
  types of 8–9
sushi rice 25–6
sushi vinegar 25–6

t
Tuna Finger Sushi 35
Tuna Rolls, Spicy 66

w
white radish "angel's hair" garnish 24
white radish garnish, shredded 24

y
Yellowtail Finger Sushi 35